When I Grow Up I Want To Be Like Donald Trump

By Chloe

Illustrations by Deanna M.

Chloe Holdings LLC
www.iwanttobeliketrump.com

Printed in the United States of America

First Edition: March 2016

ISBN-10: 0692649824
ISBN-13: 978-0692649824

DEDICATION

This book is for all the children of America
especially my sister and brother.

CONTENTS

1 MY NAME IS CHLOE   1

I WANT TO BE LIKE DONALD TRUMP BECAUSE...

2 HE IS SINCERE   5

3 HE IS A WINNER   8

4 HE DOES NOT DO DRUGS   11

5 HE IS REALLY RICH   14

6 HE IS GOING TO MAKE AMERICA GREAT AGAIN   17

When I Grow Up
I Want To Be Like
Donald Trump

1. MY NAME IS CHLOE

My name is Chloe and I am eight years old. Every evening I watch the news. I want to see what's happening in the world, and I want to be able to share it during my classroom assembly each morning.

Lately, the news has been focusing on the American elections but although I don't understand a lot about what the say, there is one man who speaks in a way that my eight year old mind can understand – Donald Trump. He is an American Billionaire.

I remember the first time I saw him. He was announcing his candidacy as President. He stood in front of 4 stately flags and said with a face so sad that "our country is in serious trouble; we don't have victories anymore."

3

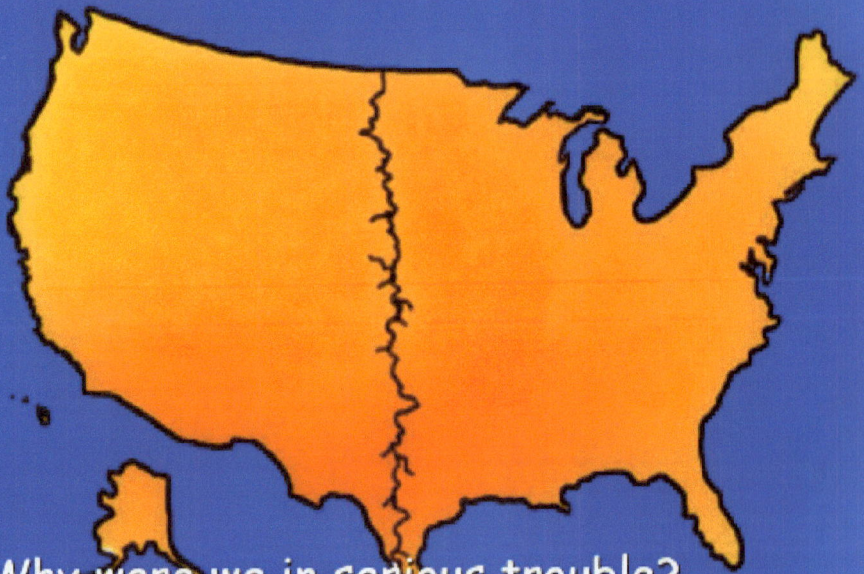

Why were we in serious trouble?
Why didn't we have victories anymore?
I wanted to know why, so I listened,
the more I listened to him, the more I
wanted our country to win, and the more
I liked him. This is why when I grow up,
I want to be like Donald Trump.

4

Truth

2. I WANT TO BE LIKE DONALD TRUMP BECAUSE HE IS SINCERE

When Donald Trump speaks, he does it from his heart. He wants to be President of America and so he has to speak a lot in public. He has to speak a lot because he has to say how he will make America great again.

5

He told us that he did not like people coming over America's border without

permission. He also said that he was going to fix the problem. Donald Trump is true and honest about what he says. When I grow up I want to be like Donald Trump because he is sincere.

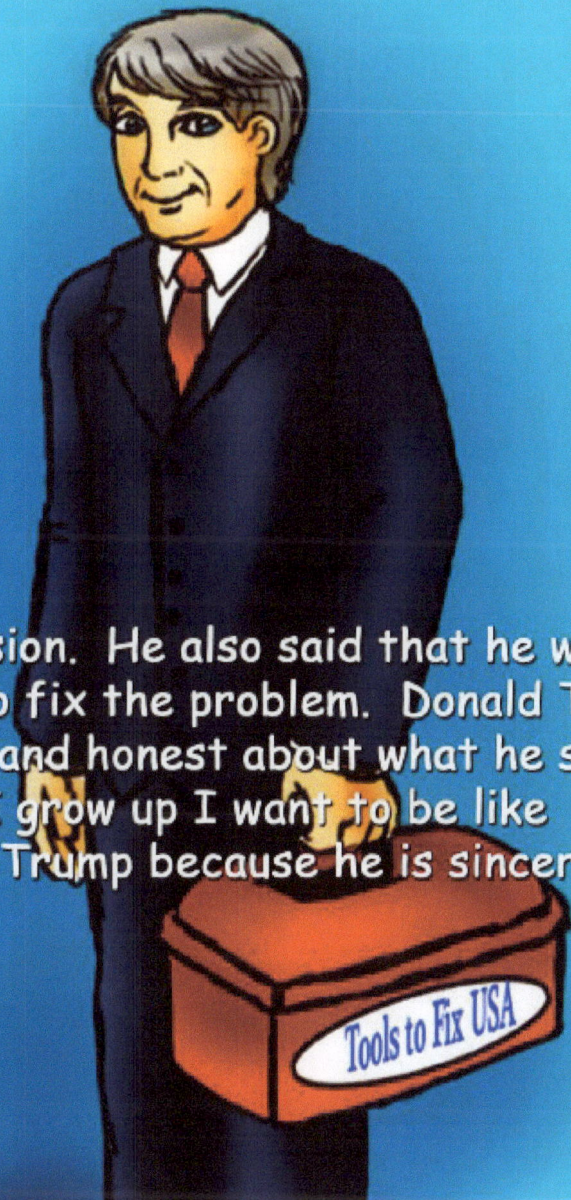

Tools to Fix USA

7

3 I WANT TO BE LIKE DONALD TRUMP BECAUSE HE IS A WINNER

Donald Trump always says that winners are not losers. He is a winner in every thing he does.

When he is making deals in New York and around the world, he never loses. He was the star of one of the best shows on television. It was called the Apprentice. Every time Donald Trump was on the show a lot of people watched.

He wants to be the next President of America.

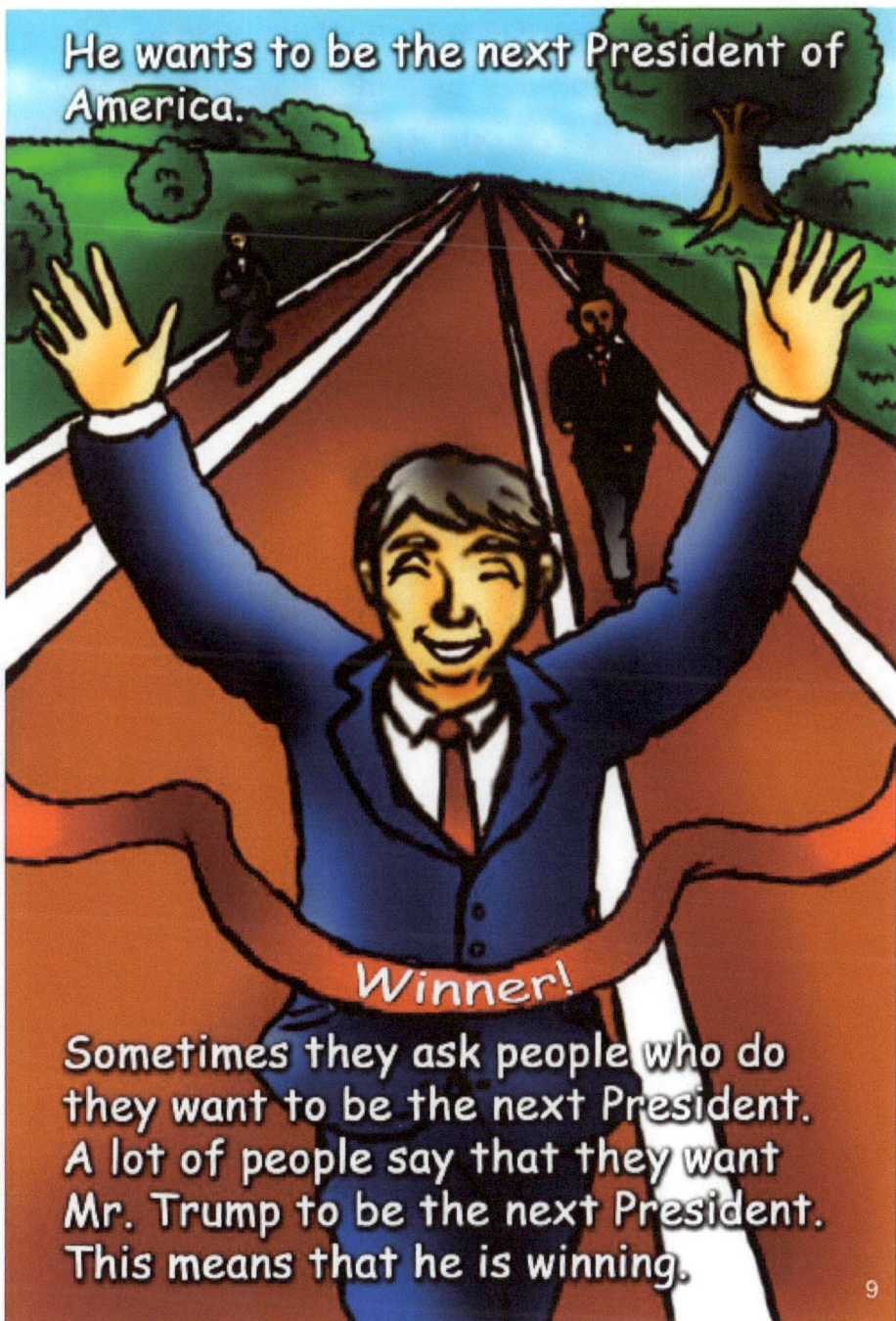

Winner!

Sometimes they ask people who do they want to be the next President. A lot of people say that they want Mr. Trump to be the next President. This means that he is winning.

9

I play games all the time with my family and I like to win. I want to always be winner. When I grow up I want to be like Donald Trump because he is a Winner.

4. I WANT TO BE LIKE DONALD TRUMP BECAUSE HE DOES NOT DO DRUGS

No
To
Drugs!

Mr. Trump says that he tells his children that there are four things they must not do. Those are (1) Do not put tattoos on your skin (2) Do not drink alcohol (3) Do not smoke and (4) Do not take drugs.

11

Drugs are bad for you. They damage your body and prevent you from being healthy. Alcohol and smoking are also bad for you.
Drugs are bad..
Donald Trump never took drugs and does not smoke or drink alcohol. I believe that is why he is living so long.

Mr. Trump had a brother who used to drink alcohol. He drank a lot of alcohol and knew that it was damaging his life, so he warned Mr. Trump not to become an alcoholic like him. Even though Mr. Trump's brother knew alcohol was bad he did not stop drinking it and now he is dead.

13

It is because he does not use drugs, smoke or drink alcohol why he is able to travel all over America and the world without getting sick.

Donald Trump is healthy and keeps his body free from drugs, cigarettes and alcohol. I want to be healthy like Donald Trump. How about you?

5.   I WANT TO BE LIKE DONALD TRUMP BECAUSE HE IS REALLY RICH

Donald Trump has a lot of money. He's not just rich, he's really rich. He lives in the State of New York. Where he lives is called Trump Tower. He lives in a very tall building in New York.

15

There is gold all over. The view is beautiful. He is the largest developer in New York. He has built several buildings and he also owns a lot of gulf courses and resorts. Mr. Trump also owns over 100 companies.

He owns even more and when Mr. Trump travels in a plane, he does it in his own plane. He owns a Helicopter and a huge 747 jet. This jet can carry 43 people. It can go as fast as five hundred miles per hour. It can travel for sixteen hours without fuel. Just like his house there is gold all over Mr. Trump's jet.

17

Mr. Trump buys what he wants when he wants. When I grow up,

I also want to be able to buy what I want without worrying about money. When I grow up, I want to have gold all over my house. Even the spoons and knives will be made of gold.

When I grow up I want to travel all over the world in my own plane.

If I am really rich like Mr. Trump, I will be able to do all that. So when I grow up I want to be like Donald Trump because he's really rich.

19

6. I WANT TO BE LIKE DONALD TRUMP BECAUSE HE IS GOING TO MAKE AMERICA GREAT AGAIN

Make America Great Again!

Donald Trump believes that America is not great anymore. He says it used to be great. He also says that America used to be admired by other countries in the world.

20

America use to make a lot of things in America but now we are making them in China and other places. This means that Americans are not able to get plenty of jobs.

This makes Donald Trump sad because he says America is no longer great but he could fix it. He is going to create more jobs for Americans and make it very safe again.

I believe that we all can play a part in making America great again. We all have to help Donald Trump make America the great country it used to be.

Make America Great Again!

TRUMP

I want all the children of America to help make this country great again. I hope everyone votes for Mr. Trump so that he can become President and make America great again.

24

ABOUT THE AUTHOR

Chloe is an eight-year old who loves Trump and believes that he can make America great again. You can email her at chloe@Iwanttobelike trump.com

www.ingramcontent.com/pod-product-compliance
Lightning Source LLC
Chambersburg PA
CBHW040346060426
42445CB00029B/23

9 7 8 0 6 9 2 6 4 9 8 2 4